Specimen Sight-Singing Tests

Grades 6-8

**The Associated Board of
the Royal Schools of Music**

Notes on the requirements

Reference must always be made to the syllabus for the year in which the examination is to be taken, in case any changes have been made to the requirements.

In the examination, the test of Singing at Sight will be accompanied by the examiner.

The test may be sung to the words provided, or on any vowel, or to sol-fa, for all grades, as the candidate prefers.

Candidates will be given a short interval of up to half a minute in which to look through and, if they wish, try out any part of the test before they are required to perform it for assessment.

1

With spirit

f

Se-mi-qua-vers run-ning thro' the mu-sic,

f

Se-mi-qua-vers run-ning thro' the mu-sic,

With spirit

f

mf

mp

mf

Dot - ted rhy - thms mark the place. Slow and fast - er___ pat - terns

mp

mf

Dot - ted rhy - thms mark the place. Slow and fast - er___ pat - terns

mp

mf

cresc.

f

fol-low one a-no-ther— set_ the pace. Watch this space!

cresc.

f

fol-low one a-no-ther— set_ the pace. Watch this space!

cresc.

f

GRADE 6

words: traditional

AB 2575

words: Inge

The val-ley rings with mirth and joy,
The val-ley rings with mirth and joy,
A - mong the hills the e-choes ring,_____ A ne - ver,
A - mong the hills the e-choes ring,_____ A ne - ver,
ne - ver_ end - ing song_____ To wel - come in the spring.
ne - ver_ end - ing song_____ To wel - come in the spring.

words: Housman

Text: extract from 'Into my heart an air that kills' (*A Shropshire Lad*) by A. E. Housman.

Reproduced by permission of The Society of Authors as the literary representative of the Estate of A. E. Housman.

GRADE 6

RC

words: Campion

GRADE 6

words: Pope

RC.

words: Hardy

Text: extract from 'In Time of "The Breaking of Nations"' (*The Complete Poems*) by Thomas Hardy.
Reproduced by permission of Macmillan Publishers Ltd.

AB 2575

words: Arnold

GRADE 7

Swift - ly turns the spin-ning wheel!

Gol - den threads so soft to feel. Rich and warm the cloth she

weaves But cold her heart when he leaves.

words: Gray

GRADE 7

words: Bridges

The day be - gins to droop, Its course is done: But no - thing, no - thing tells the place Of the set - ting sun.

Text: extract from 'Winter Nightfall' (*The Poetical Works of Robert Bridges*, OUP, 1936) by Robert Bridges.
Reproduced by permission of Oxford University Press.

    AB 2575

words: Shelley

GRADE 8

words: Chesterton

Text: extract from 'The Donkey' (*The Collected Works*) by G. K. Chesterton.
Reproduced by permission of A. P. Watt Ltd on behalf of The Royal Literary Fund.

  AB 2575

words: Goldsmith

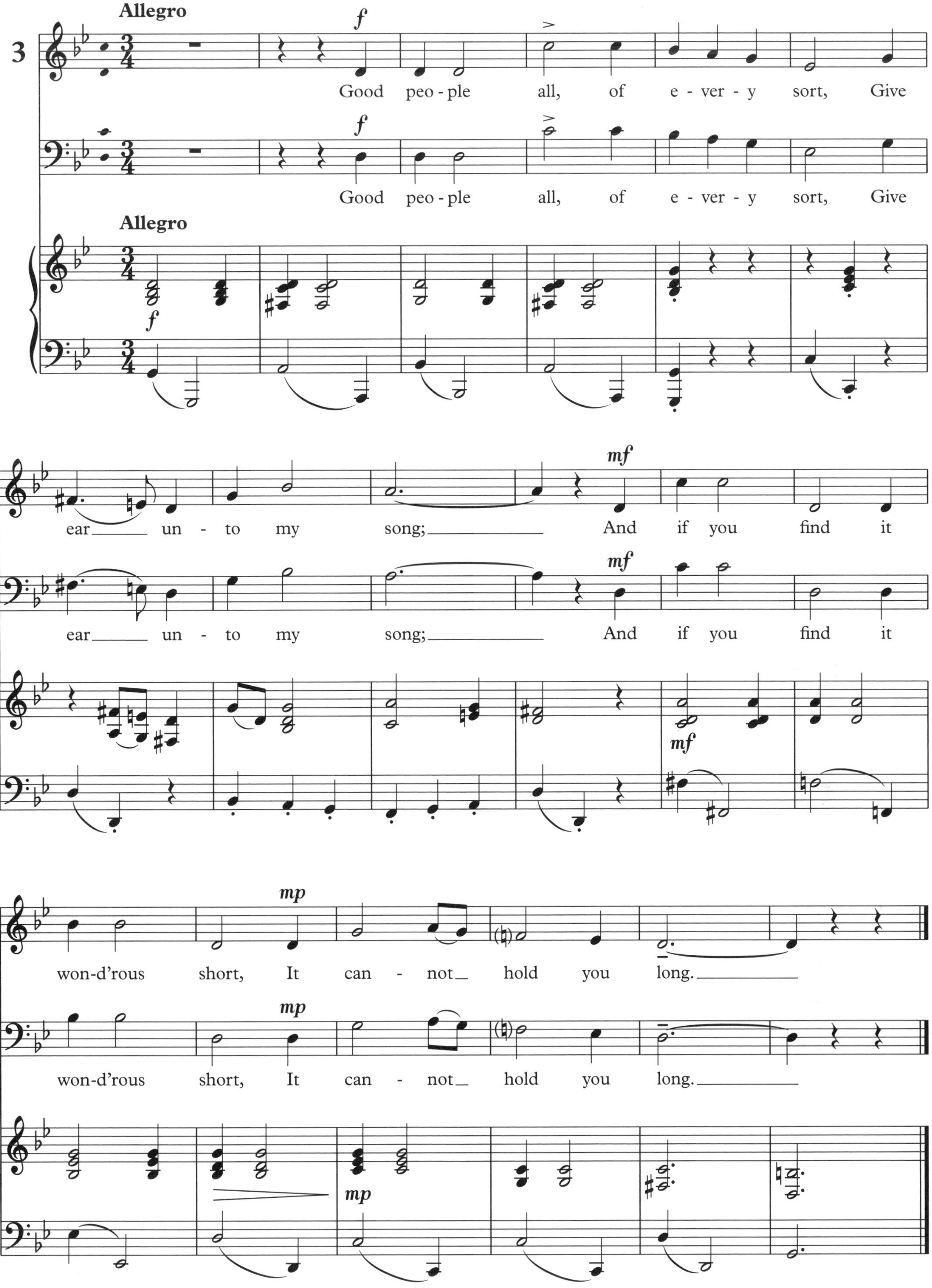

words: Field

words: Cowper

GRADE 8

words: Burns

Music and text origination by
Barnes Music Engraving Ltd, East Sussex
Printed by Caligraving Ltd, Thetford, Norfolk, England

AB 2575

4:00